My Tang's Tungled

and

other ridiculous situations

My Tang's Tungled

and
other ridiculous situations

Humorous Poems
Collected by

*Sara and John E. Brewton
and G. Meredith Blackburn III*

Illustrated by Graham Booth

Thomas Y. Crowell Company
New York

Copyright © 1973 by Sara & John E. Brewton

All rights reserved. Except for use in a review, the reproduction or utilization of this work in any form or by any electronic, mechanical, or other means, now known or hereafter invented, including xerography, photocopying, and recording, and in any information storage and retrieval system is forbidden without the written permission of the publisher. Published simultaneously in Canada by Fitzhenry & Whiteside Limited, Toronto.

Designed by Angela Foote

Manufactured in the United States of America

Library of Congress Cataloging in Publication Data

Brewton, Sara Westbrook, comp.
My tang's tungled and other ridiculous situations.

SUMMARY: A collection of humorous and nonsense poems by well-known writers.

1. Children's poetry. [1. Humorous poetry. 2. Limericks] I. Brewton, John Edmund,   joint comp. II. Blackburn, G. Meredith, joint comp. III. Booth, Graham, illus. IV. Title.
PZ8.3.B75My   821'.07   73–254
ISBN 0–690–57223–9

3 4 5 6 7 8 9 10

ACKNOWLEDGMENTS

Grateful acknowledgment is made to the following publishers, authors, and other copyright holders for permission to reprint copyrighted material:

Appleton-Century-Crofts, Inc., for "The Cantankerous 'Gator," "The Gnat and the Gnu," "A Personal Experience," and "The Provident Puffin," by Oliver Herford from *Century Magazine*, copyright © 1911, 1912, 1913, The Century Company; and "The Ingenious Little Old Man" by John Bennett and "Jorridge and Porridge" by Louise-Ayres Garnett from *St. Nicholas Magazine*, June 1897 and December 1925.

Joan Bennett, for "Peter Tatter," from *Play Way of Speech Training* by Rodney Bennett, published by Evans Brothers Limited.

Morris Bishop, for "Song of the Pop-Bottlers," from *A Bowl of Bishop* by Morris Bishop, Dial Press, copyright © 1954. Originally published in *The New Yorker*.

iv

v

Books Compiled by John E. Brewton

Under the Tent of the Sky
Gaily We Parade
Poetry Time

With Sara Brewton:

Christmas Bells Are Ringing
Bridled with Rainbows
Sing a Song of Seasons
Birthday Candles Burning Bright
Laughable Limericks
America Forever New
    A BOOK OF POEMS
Shrieks at Midnight
    MACABRE POEMS, EERIE AND HUMOROUS
Index to Children's Poetry
Index to Children's Poetry
    FIRST SUPPLEMENT
Index to Children's Poetry
    SECOND SUPPLEMENT

With Sara Brewton and G. Meredith Blackburn III

Index to Poetry for Children and Young People

Contents

THE KING OF HEARTS

"I like this book," said the King of Hearts.
"It makes me laugh the way it starts!"

"I like it also!" said his Mother.
So they sat down and read it to each other.

William Jay Smith

My Tang's Tungled

Tongue twisters twist tongues twisted
Trying to untangle twisted tangles:
My tang's tungled now.

AUTHOR   UNKNOWN

TWO WITCHES

There was a witch
The witch had an itch
The itch was so itchy it
Gave her a twitch.

Another witch
Admired the twitch
So she started twitching
Though she had no itch.

Now both of them twitch
So it's hard to tell which
Witch has the itch and
Which witch has the twitch.

Alexander Resnikoff

JUMBLE JINGLE

Pick up a stick up,
    A stick up now pick;
Let me hear you say that
    Nine times, *quick!*

Laura E. Richards

ELETELEPHONY

Once there was an elephant,
Who tried to use the telephant—
No! no! I mean an elephone
Who tried to use the telephone—
(Dear me! I am not certain quite
That even now I've got it right.)

Howe'er it was, he got his trunk
Entangled in the telephunk;
The more he tried to get it free,
The louder buzzed the telephee—
(I fear I'd better drop the song
Of elephop and telephong!)

Laura E. Richards

SHUT THE SHUTTER

"Go, my son, and shut the shutter,"
This I heard a mother utter.
"Shutter's shut," the boy did mutter,
"I can't shut 'er any shutter."

Author Unknown

SONG OF THE POP-BOTTLERS

Pop bottles pop-bottles
  In pop shops;
The pop-bottles Pop bottles
  Poor Pop drops.

When Pop drops pop-bottles,
  Pop-bottles plop!
Pop-bottle-tops topple!
  Pop mops slop!

Stop! Pop'll drop bottle!
  Stop, Pop, stop!
When Pop bottles pop-bottles
  Pop-bottles pop!

Morris Bishop

YOU'VE NO NEED TO LIGHT A
NIGHT LIGHT

You've no need to light a night light
On a light night like tonight,
For a night light's light's a slight light,
And tonight's a night that's light.
When a night's light, like tonight's light,
It is really not quite right
To light night lights with their slight lights
On a light night like tonight.

Author Unknown

IF A DOCTOR IS DOCTORING A DOCTOR

If a doctor is doctoring a doctor,
Does the doctor doing the doctoring
Doctor the doctor being doctored
The way the doctor being doctored
Wants to be doctored,
Or does the doctor doctoring the doctor
Doctor the doctor being doctored
The way the doctoring doctor usually doctors?
Yes, the doctor doing the doctoring
Doctors the doctor being doctored
The way he, the doctoring doctor,
Thinks the doctor being doctored
Should be doctored.

Author Unknown

I SAW ESAU

I saw Esau kissing Kate.
Fact is, we all three saw.
I saw Esau, he saw me,
And she saw I saw Esau.

Author Unknown

MOSES

Moses supposes his toeses are roses,
But Moses supposes erroneously;
For nobody's toeses are posies of roses
As Moses supposes his toeses to be.

Author Unknown

A SKUNK SAT ON A STUMP

A skunk sat on a stump.
The skunk thinked
the stump stunk,
but the stump thunk
the skunk stunk.

Author Unknown

SAY, DID YOU SAY?

Say, did you say, or did you not say
What I said you said?
For it is said that you said
That you did not say
What I said you said.
Now if you say that you did not say
What I said you said,
Then what do you say you did say instead
Of what I said you said?

Author Unknown

A FLEA AND A FLY

A flea and a fly in a flue
Were caught, so what could they do?
   Said the fly, "Let us flee."
   "Let us fly," said the flea.
So they flew through a flaw in the flue.

Author Unknown

THE OLD SCHOOL SCOLD

The old school scold sold
The school coal scuttle:
If the old school scold sold
The school coal scuttle,
The school should scold
And scuttle the old school scold.

Author Unknown

THE TOOTING TUTOR

A tutor who tooted a flute
Tried to tutor two tooters to toot
   Said the two to the tutor,
   "Is it harder to toot, or
To tutor two tooters to toot?"

Author Unknown

SHE SELLS SEASHELLS

She sells seashells on the seashore.
The shells she sells are seashells, I'm sure.
So if she sells seashells on the seashore,
I'm sure she sells seashore shells.

Author Unknown

WHEN A JOLLY YOUNG FISHER

When a jolly young fisher named Fisher
Went fishing for fish in a fissure,
    A fish, with a grin,
    Pulled the fisherman in.
Now they're fishing the fissure for Fisher.

Author Unknown

THE BAKER'S REPLY TO THE
NEEDLE PEDDLER

I need not your needles, they're needless to me,
For kneading of needles were needless, you see,
But did my neat trousers but need to be kneed,
I then should have need of your needles indeed.

Author Unknown

WHICH SWITCH FOR IPSWICH?

Which switch is the switch, Miss, for Ipswich?
It's the Ipswich switch which I require.
Which switch is the switch, Miss, for Ipswich?
You switched me on the wrong wire.
You switched me on Norwich, not Ipswich,
So now to prevent further hitch,
If you'll tell me, Miss, which switch is Norwich
And which switch is Ipswich,
I'll know which switch is which.

Author Unknown

PETER PRANGLE

Peter Prangle,
The prickly prangly pear picker,
Picked three pecks
Of prangly prickly pears, from
The prickly prangly pear trees
On the pleasant prairies.

Author Unknown

TOUCANS TWO

Whatever one toucan can do
is sooner done by toucans two,
and three toucans (it's very true)
can do much more than two can do.

And toucans numbering two plus two can
manage more than all the zoo can.
In short, there is no toucan who can
do what four or three or two can.

Jack Prelutsky

A TREE TOAD

A tree toad loved a she-toad
That lived up in a tree.
He was a two-toed tree toad
While a three-toed toad was she.
The he-toad tree toad tried to gain
The she-toad's friendly nod.
For the two-toed tree toad loved the ground
That the three-toed tree toad trod.
The two-toed tree toad tried in vain
But couldn't please her whim,
For from her tree toad bower
With her she-toad power
The three-toed tree toad vetoed him.

Author Unknown

PETER TATTER

Peter Tatter popped his batter
Pudding on a painted platter,
Peter Tatter ate that batter,
Batter makes Pete Tatter fatter.

Rodney Bennett

CELIA

Celia sat beside the seaside,
Quite beside herself was she
For beside her on the leeside
No one sat beside her, see?

Author Unknown

The Folk Who
Live in Backward Town

The folk who live in Backward Town
Are inside out and upside down.
They wear their hats inside their heads
And go to sleep beneath their beds.
They only eat the apple peeling
And take their walks across the ceiling.

MARY ANN HOBERMAN

TOO POLITE

Broad met Stout
At the gate, and each
Was too polite to brush past.
"After you!" said Broad.
"After you!" said Stout.
They got in a dither
And went through together
And both
   stuck
      fast.

Ian Serraillier

THE INGENIOUS LITTLE OLD MAN

A little old man of the sea
Went out in a boat for a sail:
The water came in
Almost up to his chin
And he had nothing with which to bail.
But this little old man of the sea
Just drew out his jack-knife so stout,
And a hole with its blade
In the bottom he made,
So that all of the water ran out.

John Bennett

from AN ODD FELLOW

There was one who was famed for the number of things
    He forgot when he entered the ship;
His umbrella, his watch, all his jewels and rings,
    And the clothes he had bought for the trip.

He had forty-two boxes, all carefully packed,
    With his name painted clearly on each;
But, since he omitted to mention the fact,
    They were all left behind on the beach.

The loss of his clothes hardly mattered, because
    He had seven coats on when he came,
With three pairs of boots—but the worst of it was,
    He had wholly forgotten his name.

He would answer to "Hi!" or to any loud cry,
    Such as "Fry me!" or "Fritter my wig!"
To "What-you-may-call-um!" or "What-was-his-name!"
    But especially "Thing-um-a-jig!"

Lewis Carroll

MR. KARTOFFEL

Mr. Kartoffel's a whimsical man;
He drinks his beer from a watering-can,
And for no good reason that I can see
He fills his pockets with china tea.
He parts his hair with a knife and fork
And takes his ducks for a Sunday walk.
Says he, "If my wife and I should choose
To wear our stockings outside our shoes,
Plant tulip-bulbs in the baby's pram
And eat tobacco instead of jam,
And fill the bath with cauliflowers,
That's nobody's business at all but ours."
Says Mrs. K. "I may choose to travel
With a sack of grass or a sack of gravel,
Or paint my toes, one black, one white,
Or sit on a bird's nest half the night—
But whatever I do that is rum or rare,
I rather think that it's my affair.
So fill up your pockets with stamps and string,
And let us be ready for anything!"
Says Mr. K. to his whimsical wife,
"How can we face the storms of life,
Unless we are ready for anything?
So if you've provided the stamps and string,
Let us pump up the saddle and harness the horse
And fill him with carrots and custard and sauce,
Let us leap on him lightly and give him a shove
And it's over the sea and away, my love!"

James Reeves

A MODERN BALLAD
The Ups and Downs of the Elevator Car

The elevator car in the elevator shaft,
Complained of the buzzer, complained of the draft.
It said it felt carsick as it rose and fell,
It said it had a headache from the ringing of the bell.

"There is spring in the air," sighed the elevator car.
Said the elevator man, "You are well-off where you are."
The car paid no attention but it frowned an ugly frown

<pre>
                            when
                    up   it
                going   should
        started   be
     it   going
And   down.
</pre>

Down flashed the signal, but *up* went the car.
The elevator man cried, "You are going much too far!"
Said the elevator car, "I'm doing no such thing.
I'm through with buzzers buzzing. I'm looking for the spring!"

Then the elevator man began to shout and call
And all the people came running through the hall.
The elevator man began to call and shout.
"The car won't stop! Let me out! Let me out!"

On went the car past the penthouse door.
On went the car up one flight more.
On went the elevator till it came to the top.
On went the elevator, and it would not stop!

Right through the roof went the man and the car.
And nobody knows where the two of them are!
(Nobody knows but everyone cares,
Wearily, drearily climbing the stairs!)

Now on a summer evening when you see a shooting star
Fly through the air, perhaps it *is*—that elevator car!

Caroline D. Emerson

J'S THE JUMPING JAY-WALKER

J's the jumping Jay-walker,
   A sort of human jeep.
He crosses where the lights are red.
   Before he looks, he'll leap!
Then many a wheel
Begins to squeal,
   And many a brake to slam.
He turns your knees to jelly
   And the traffic into jam.

Phyllis McGinley

OLD QUIN QUEERIBUS

Old Quin Queeribus—
　　He loved his garden so,
He wouldn't have a rake around,
　　A shovel or a hoe.

For each potato's eyes he bought
　　Fine spectacles of gold,
And mufflers for the corn, to keep
　　Its ears from getting cold.

On every head of lettuce green—
　　What do you think of that?—
And every head of cabbage, too,
　　He tied a garden hat.

Old Quin Queeribus
　　He loved his garden so,
He couldn't eat his growing things,
　　He only let them grow!

Nancy Byrd Turner

MISTER BEERS

This is Mister Beers;
    And for forty-seven years
He's been digging in his garden like a miner.
    He isn't planting seeds
    Nor scratching up the weeds,
He's trying to bore a tunnel down to China.

Hugh Lofting

JORRIDGE AND PORRIDGE

Jorridge and Porridge
Went out for a walk.
Said Porridge to Jorridge:
"I wish you would talk."

Said Jorridge to Porridge:
"I've nothing to say."
So, silent as ever,
They wended their way.

Louise Ayres Garnett

SCALLYWAG AND GOLLYWOG

Scallywag and Gollywog
Took their bag aboard a log
    And started off to cross the ocean blue.
They're still at sea, I have no doubt,
For all they do is fight about
    Which shall be the Captain, which the crew.

Hugh Lofting

THE ABSENT-MINDED MAN

I know an absent-minded man.
  He's neither stout nor thin.
He just forgets why he went out
  And so he comes back in.

I know an absent-minded man.
  He's neither thin nor stout.
He just forgets why he came in
  And so he goes back out.

Georgia H. MacPherson

This Little Morsel

But this little morsel of morsels here—
Just what it is is not quite clear:
It might be pudding, it might be meat,
Cold, or hot, or salt, or sweet;
Baked, or roasted, or broiled, or fried;
Bare, or frittered, or puddinged, or pied;
Cooked in a saucepan, jar, or pan—
But it's all the same to Elizabeth Ann.
For when one's hungry it doesn't much matter
So long as there's something on one's platter.

WALTER DE LA MARE

THE TOASTER

A silver-scaled Dragon with jaws flaming red
Sits at my elbow and toasts my bread.
I hand him fat slices, and then, one by one,
He hands them back when he sees they are done.

William Jay Smith

CRUEL MISS NEWELL

Miss Seraphina Martha Newell
Was thought by some to be quite cruel.
  And shall I tell you why?

On Saturdays she used to bake
The pastry cakes, the tasty cake,
  And pastry known as pie.

To watch her was a fearsome sight!
She *beat* the eggs, both yolk and white;
She *whipped* the cream with all her might,
And *stoned* the raisins with delight!

That's why Miss Seraphina Newell
Was thought by some to be quite cruel.

Charles Battell Loomis

THE WORM

When the earth is turned in spring
The worms are fat as anything.

And birds come flying all around
To eat the worms right off the ground.

They like worms just as much as I
Like bread and milk and apple pie.

And once, when I was very young,
I put a worm right on my tongue.

I didn't like the taste a bit,
And so I didn't swallow it.

But oh, it makes my Mother squirm
Because she *thinks* I ate that worm!

Ralph Bergengren

THE CANTANKEROUS 'GATOR

There was a cantankerous 'gator
For whom 'twas no pleasure to cater.
    If he happened to find
    No dish to his mind,
He would like as not swallow the waiter.

Oliver Herford

MY HOUSE

My house is made of Graham bread,
    Except the ceiling's made of white;
Of angel cake I make my bed—
    I eat my pillow every night!

Gelett Burgess

I EAT MY PEAS WITH HONEY

I eat my peas with honey;
I've done it all my life.
It makes the peas taste funny,
But it keeps them on the knife.

Author Unknown

THE PROVIDENT PUFFIN

There once was a provident puffin
Who ate all the fish he could stuff in.
　　Said he, " 'Tis my plan
　　To eat when I can:
When there's nuffin' to eat I eat nuffin'."

Oliver Herford

SOME COOK!

Johnny made a custard
In the pepper pot.
Flavored it with mustard,
Put in quite a lot
Of garlic fried in olive oil,
Brought the custard to a boil,
Ate it up and burned his tongue—

You shouldn't cook when you're too young.

John Ciardi

THE SILVER FISH

While fishing in the blue lagoon,
I caught a lovely silver fish,
And he spoke to me, "My boy," quoth he,
"Please set me free and I'll grant your wish;
A kingdom of wisdom? A palace of gold?
Or all the fancies your mind can hold?"
And I said, "O.K.," and I set him free,
But he laughed at me as he swam away,
And left me whispering my wish
Into a silent sea.

Today I caught that fish again
(That lovely silver prince of fishes),
And once again he offered me,
If I would only set him free,
Any one of a number of wishes,
If I would throw him back to the fishes.

He was delicious!

Shel Silverstein

THE MAN IN THE ONION BED

I met a man in an onion bed.
He was crying so hard his eyes were red.
And the tears ran off the end of his nose
As he ate his way down the onion rows.

He ate and he cried, but for all his tears
He sang: "Sweet onions, oh my dears!
I love you, I do, and you love me,
But you make me as sad as a man can be."

"Why are you crying?" I asked. And he
Stopped his singing and looked at me.
"I love my onions, I do," he said,
"And I hate to pull them out of bed.
And wouldn't it make *you* want to weep
To eat them up while they're still asleep?"

"Then why don't you wake them?"
                          "Ah," he said,
"Onions are best when they're still in bed!"
And he cried and he ate and he ate and he cried
Till row by row and side to side
He ate till there were no more, then sat
And started to cry again for that.

He cried till his coat and shoes were wet.
For all I know, he is crying yet.

John Ciardi

BABY KATE

Darling little Baby Kate
Poured her broth on father's pate.
Father hollered, "Hey, you goop!
That's my noodle in your soup!"

Joseph S. Newman

THERE WAS A YOUNG LADY FROM CORK

There was a young lady from Cork
Who went at her soup with a fork.
   When her parents looked pained
   She proudly explained,
"That's the way they eat soup in New York."

Ogden Nash

Family Fun

Everyone grumbled. The sky was grey.
We had nothing to do and nothing to say.
We were nearing the end of a dismal day,
And there seemed to be nothing beyond,

      THEN
    Daddy fell into the pond!

ALFRED NOYES

SIT UP WHEN YOU SIT DOWN!

Someone about as big as a bump
Sat down to breakfast all a-slump
With his head in his hands and his chin in the plate.
"Sit up!" I said. "Yes, you. Sit *straight!*
Sit *up* I say!" I saw him frown.
"Sit up," I said, "when you sit down!"

He let out a *giggle*. He let out a roar.
He almost rolled around on the floor.
"How can I?" he said when he saw me frown,
"How can I sit *up* when I sit *down?*"

Well, what could I do? It was getting late.
And he hadn't eaten a thing from his plate.
I had to show him. I had to be quick
Or he'd miss school. So I got a stick . . .

And did I beat him? Goodness, no!
He took one look and he seemed to know
Just how to sit up when he sits down.
And now he's the very best boy in town!

John Ciardi

GRANDPA DROPPED HIS GLASSES

Grandpa dropped his glasses once
In a pot of dye,
And when he put them on again
He saw a purple sky.
Purple birds were rising up
From a purple hill,
Men were grinding purple cider
At a purple mill.
Purple Adeline was playing
With a purple doll,
Little purple dragon flies
Were crawling up the wall.
And at the supper-table
He got crazy as a loon
From eating purple apple dumplings
With a purple spoon.

Leroy F. Jackson

BETWIXT AND BETWEEN

Betwixt and Between were two betwins,
Their father's name was Twoddle.
They've been alike as a pair of pins
Since they could scarcely toddle.

Hugh Lofting

AUNT JANE

Aunt Jane's in such a hurry,
She makes us all perplexed,
And when I'm in one moment,
She's always in the next.

When I ride a camel,
She talks of getting down;
And when I start to paddle,
She speaks of boys who drown;

She talks about the doctor,
When cakes are going free;
And when I stroke an elephant,
She says I'll catch a flea.

And she is always thinking
Of dull times to come,
"Time for rest," and "time for bed,"
And "time for going home."

Aunt Jane's in such a hurry,
She makes us all perplexed;
And when I'm in one moment,
She's always in the next.

Herbert Asquith

BIRTHDAYS

We had waffles-with-syrup for breakfast,
    As many as we could hold;
And I had some presents extra,
    Because I am nine years old.

I've thanked everyone for my presents,
    And kissed 'em, and now that that's done
The family's all ready to do things,
    Whatever I think would be fun.

When Timothy had his birthday
    We went to the circus, and Tim
Made friends with the seals and the monkeys
    And a real clown winked at him.

And Dorothy chose a picnic
    On the shore of a little lake,
With tadpoles, and buns, and diving,
    And a four-layer birthday cake.

And now that it's my turn for choosing,
    I'm going to ask if we might
Take all of our family of rabbits
    To bed with us just for tonight.

Marchette Chute

THE QUEENS' RHYME

The King has married two wives,
    each a Prince's daughter.
"I'm a Queen, and you're a Queen
    so who's to fetch the water?"

Ian Serraillier

MUMPS

I had a feeling in my neck,
And on the sides were two big bumps;
I couldn't swallow anything
At all because I had the mumps.

And Mother tied it with a piece,
And then she tied up Will and John,
And no one else but Dick was left
That didn't have a mump rag on.

He teased at us and laughed at us,
And said, whenever he went by,
"It's vinegar and lemon drops
And pickles!" just to make us cry.

But Tuesday Dick was very sad
And cried because his neck was sore,
And not a one said sour things
To anybody any more.

Elizabeth Madox Roberts

THE TWINS

In form and feature, face and limb,
    I grew so like my brother,
That folks got taking me for him,
    And each for one another.
It puzzled all our kith and kin,
    It reached an awful pitch;
For one of us was born a twin,
    Yet not a soul knew which.

One day (to make the matter worse),
    Before our names were fixed,
As we were being washed by nurse
    We got completely mixed;
And thus, you see, by Fate's decree,
    (Or rather nurse's whim),
My brother John got christened *me*,
    And I got christened *him*.

This fatal likeness even dogg'd
    My footsteps when at school,
And I was always getting flogg'd,
    For John turned out a fool.
I put this question hopelessly
    To every one I knew—
What *would* you do, if you were me,
    To prove that you were *you*?

Our close resemblance turned the tide
   Of my domestic life;
For somehow my intended bride
   Became my brother's wife.
In short, year after year the same
   Absurd mistake went on;
And when I died—the neighbors came
   And buried brother John!

Henry S. Leigh

A PARTY

On Willy's birthday, as you see,
These little boys have come to tea.
But, oh! how very sad to tell!
They have not been behaving well.
For ere they took a single bite,
They all began to scold and fight.

The little boy whose name was Ned,
He wanted jelly on his bread;
The little boy whose name was Sam,
He vowed he would have damson jam;
The little boy whose name was Phil
Said, "I'll have honey! Yes—I—WILL!"

BUT—
The little boy whose name was Paul,
While they were quarrelling, ate it all.

Laura E. Richards

CHOOSING SHOES

New shoes, new shoes,
Red and pink and blue shoes,
Tell me, what would *you* choose,
    If they'd let us buy?

Buckle-shoes, bow shoes,
Pretty pointy-toe shoes,
Strappy, cappy, low shoes;
  Let's have some to try.

Bright shoes, white shoes,
Dandy-dance-by-night shoes—
Perhaps-a-little-tight shoes,
  Like some? So would I.

        BUT
Flat shoes, fat shoes,
Stump-along-like-that shoes,
Wipe-them-on-the-mat shoes,
  That's the sort they'll buy.

                        ffrida Wolfe

UNCLE SIMON AND UNCLE JIM

Uncle Simon he
Clumb up a tree
To see
What he could see,
When presentlee
Uncle Jim
Clumb up beside of him
And squatted down by he.

                    Artemus Ward

47

THE CHRISTMAS EXCHANGE

When Bill gives me a book, I know
It's just the book he wanted, so
When I give him a ping-pong set,
He's sure it's what I hoped to get.

Then after Christmas we arrange
A little Christmas Gift Exchange;
I give the book to him, and he
Gives back the ping-pong set to me.

So each gives twice—and that is pleasant—
To get the truly-wanted present.

Arthur Guiterman

PRESENTS

I wanted a rifle for Christmas,
   I wanted a bat and a ball,
I wanted some skates and a bicycle,
   But I didn't want mittens at all.

     I wanted a whistle
       And I wanted a kite.
     I wanted a pocketknife
       That shut up tight.
     I wanted some boots
       And I wanted a kit,
But I didn't want mittens one little bit.

I told them I didn't like mittens,
    I told them as plain as plain.
I told them I didn't WANT mittens,
    And they've given me mittens again!

Marchette Chute

DADDY FELL INTO THE POND

Everyone grumbled. The sky was grey.
We had nothing to do and nothing to say.
We were nearing the end of a dismal day,
And there seemed to be nothing beyond,

      THEN
Daddy fell into the pond!

And everyone's face grew merry and bright,
And Timothy danced for sheer delight.
"Give me the camera, quick, oh quick!
He's crawling out of the duckweed." *Click!*

Then the gardener suddenly slapped his knee,
And doubled up, shaking silently,
And the ducks all quacked as if they were daft,
And it sounded as if the old drake laughed.

O, there wasn't a thing that didn't respond

      WHEN
Daddy fell into the pond!

Alfred Noyes

Animal Adventures

OFF TO YAKIMA

Nipper and the Nanny-Goat,
Piggy and the Pup
Started off to Yakima
To drink the river up.

When they got to Yakima
They couldn't drink a sup,
For the silly little simpletons
Forgot to bring a cup

LEROY F. JACKSON

ADVICE FROM AN ELDERLY MOUSE

If you happen to meet
With a cat some day,
It's common sense
To get out of her way.
   It's common sense,
      Plain common sense,
         To scamper, well out of her way!

It's common sense
But it isn't fear,
For always remember
The mouse, my dear,
   Remember the mouse,
      Our ancestor mouse,
         Who rescued a Lion, my dear.

The Lion was caught
In a hunter's net,
He struggled and roared
But he couldn't get
   Out of the net,
      The terrible net,
         Until he was helped by a mouse he had met.

If a mouse can save
A Lion, it's clear
When we run away
It isn't through fear,
   Wisdom, not fear,
      Not fear, my dear,
         Will suggest when it's best to get out of here!

Elizabeth Coatsworth

THE SNAIL'S DREAM

A snail, who had a way, it seems,
Of dreaming very curious dreams,
Once dreamed he was—you'll never guess!—
The Lightning Limited Express!

Oliver Herford

HOSPITALITY

Said a snake to a frog with a wrinkled skin,
"As I notice, dear, that your dress is thin,
And a rain is coming,
    I'll take you in."

John Banister Tabb

THE PUZZLED CENTIPEDE

A centipede was happy quite,
Until a frog in fun
Said, "Pray, which leg comes after which?"
This raised her mind to such a pitch,
She lay distracted in the ditch
Considering how to run.

Author Unknown

LAUGHING TIME

It was laughing time, and the tall Giraffe
Lifted his head, and began to laugh:

Ha! Ha!   Ha! Ha!

And the Chimpanzee on the ginkgo tree
Swung merrily down with a *Tee Hee Hee:*

Hee! Hee!   Hee! Hee!

"It's certainly not against the law!"
Croaked Justice Crow with a loud guffaw:

Haw! Haw!   Haw! Haw!

The dancing Bear who could never say "No"
Waltzed up and down on the tip of his toe:

Ho! Ho!   Ho! Ho!

The Donkey daintily took his paw,
And around they went: Hee-Haw! Hee-Haw!

Hee-Haw!   Hee-Haw!

The Moon had to smile as it started to climb;
All over the world it was laughing time!

Ho! Ho!   Ho! Ho!   Hee-Haw!   Hee-Haw!
Hee! Hee!   Hee! Hee!   Ha! Ha!   Ha! Ha!

William Jay Smith

THE SKUNK

Jacko the Skunk, in black and white,
Walked up the road one summer night,
And there he met in gold and green,
The biggest toad he'd ever seen.

Said Mr. Skunk to Mr. Toad,
"This is a strictly private road.
You need no sign-post, I suppose?"
"No," said the Toad, "I have my nose."

"Wazzat?" "Oh my! Gee whiz! Gee whiz!
A private road? It surely is.
Truer word was never said.
Phew!" cried Mr. Toad—and fled.

Alfred Noyes

THE GNAT AND THE GNU

"How absurd," said the gnat to the gnu,
"To spell your queer name as you do!"
   "For the matter of that,"
   Said the gnu to the gnat,
"That's just how I feel about you."

Oliver Herford

THE SHIP OF RIO

There was a ship of Rio
  Sailed out into the blue,
And nine and ninety monkeys
  Were all her jovial crew.
From bo'sun to the cabin boy,
  From quarter to caboose,
There weren't a stitch of calico
  To breech 'em—tight or loose;
From spar to deck, from deck to keel,
  From barnacle to shroud,
There weren't one pair of reach-me-downs
  To all that jabbering crowd.
But wasn't it a gladsome sight,
  When roared the deep-sea gales,
To see them reef her fore and aft,
  A-swinging by their tails!
Oh, wasn't it a gladsome sight,
  When glassy calm did come,
To see them squatting tailor-wise
  Around a keg of rum!
Oh, wasn't it a gladsome sight,
  When in she sailed to land,
To see them all a-scampering skip
  For nuts across the sand!

Walter De La Mare

CROCODILE

The Crocodile wept bitter tears,
   And when I asked him why,
He said: "I weep because the years
   Go far too quickly by!

"I weep because of oranges,
   I weep because of pears,
Because of broken door hinges,
   And dark and crooked stairs.

"I weep because of black shoestrings,
   I weep because of socks,
I weep because I can't do things
   Like dance and shadowbox.

"I weep because the deep blue sea
   Washes the sand in a pile;
I weep because, as you can see,
   I've never learned to smile!"

"To weep like that cannot be fun,
   My reptile friend," I said;
"Your nose, though long, will run and run,
   Your eyes, though wide, be red.

"Why must you so give way to grief?
   You *could* smile if you chose;
Here, take this pocket handkerchief
   And wipe your eyes and nose.

"Come, laugh because of oranges,
   And laugh because of pears,
Because of broken door hinges,
   And dark and crooked stairs.

"Come, laugh because of black shoestrings,
    And laugh because of socks,
And laugh because you *can* do things
    Like dance and shadowbox.

"Come, laugh because it feels so good—
    It's not against the law.
Throw open, as a reptile should,
    Your green and shining jaw!"

The Crocodile he thought awhile
    Till things seemed not so black;
He smiled, and I returned his smile,
    He smiled, and I smiled back.

He took an orange and a pear;
    He took shoestrings and socks,
And tossing them into the air,
    Began to waltz and box.

The animals came, and they were gay:
    The Bobcat danced with the Owl;
The Bat brought tea on a bamboo tray
    To the Yak and Guinea Fowl.

The Monkeys frolicked in the street;
    The Lion, with a smile,
Came proudly down the steps to greet
    The happy Crocodile!

William Jay Smith

TONY THE TURTLE

Tony was a Turtle,
  Very much at ease,
Swimming in the sunshine
  Through the summer seas,
And feeding on the fishes,
Irrespective of their wishes,
With a "By your leave" and "Thank you"
  And a gentlemanly squeeze.

Tony was a Turtle
  Who loved a civil phrase;
Anxious and obliging,
  Sensitive to praise.
And to hint that he was snappy
Made him thoroughly unhappy;
For Tony was a Turtle
  With most engaging ways.

Tony was a Turtle
  Who thought, before he fed,
Of other people's comfort,
  And as he ate them said:
"If I seem a little grumpy,
It is *not* that you are lumpy."
For Tony was a Turtle
  Delicately bred.

E. V. Rieu

A PERSONAL EXPERIENCE

A puppy whose hair was so flowing
There really was no means of knowing
    Which end was his head
    Once stopped me and said,
"Please, sir, am I coming or going?"

Oliver Herford

AN INCONVENIENCE

To his cousin the Bat
Squeaked the envious Rat,
"How fine to be able to fly!"
Tittered she, "Leather wings
Are convenient things;
But nothing *to sit on* have I."

John Banister Tabb

THE TOAD

I found me a hoptoad
Sitting in the yard.
I tried to watch him,
But watching him was hard.
He hopped in the road
With one big hop,
And I called out, "Toad,
Stop!
Stop!"

"Toad," I yelled,
"Get out of the road.
Here comes a truck
With a mighty heavy load!"

The truck came a-racketing
And roaring on,
And just as I thought:
"There's a good toad gone,"
S l o w l y
The toad hopped onto the lawn.

The toad acted sleepy
As the truck went by,
And while he rested
And blinked a beady eye,
My ears heard a whirring,
And my nose smelled gas,
And up came Willie,
Gaily mowing grass.

The wheels of the power-mower
Never once slowed;
And—suddenly scared—
I shouted, "Toad,
Hurry up.
Hop!
Or you'll get mowed!"

"A mower," I told him,
Trying hard to talk,
"Can grind up a toad
Like a dandelion stalk."
The toad peered over
A bud of white clover
And s l o w l y
Hopped on the flagstone walk.

That was the second thing
But still not the last.
After a minute
A puppy lolloped past.
I drove off the puppy,
And I scatted a cat,
And I took the toad
To the woods
After that.

I like being helpful,
And I'm no quitter,
But *that* toad needed
A baby sitter.

                    Kaye Starbird

FORGIVEN

I found a little beetle, so that Beetle was his name,
And I called him Alexander and he answered just the same.
I put him in a match-box, and I kept him all the day . . .
And Nanny let my beetle out—

    Yes, Nanny let my beetle out—
      She went and let my beetle out—
        And Beetle ran away.

She said she didn't mean it, and I never said she did,
She said she wanted matches and she just took off the lid,
She said that she was sorry, but it's difficult to catch
An excited sort of beetle you've mistaken for a match.

She said that she was sorry, and I really mustn't mind,
As there's lots and lots of beetles which she's certain we could
    find,
If we looked about the garden for the holes where beetles
    hid—
And we'd get another match-box and write BEETLE on the
    lid.

We went to all the places which a beetle might be near,
And we made the sort of noises which a beetle likes to hear,
And I saw a kind of something, and I gave a sort of shout:
"A beetle-house and Alexander Beetle coming out!"

It was Alexander Beetle I'm as certain as can be
And he had a sort of look as if he thought it must be ME,
And he had a sort of look as if he thought he ought to say:
"I'm very very sorry that I tried to run away."

And Nanny's very sorry too for you-know-what-she-did,
And she's writing ALEXANDER very blackly on the lid.
So Nan and Me are friends, because it's difficult to catch
An excited Alexander you've mistaken for a match.

A. A. Milne

OLD HOGAN'S GOAT

Old Hogan's goat was feeling fine,
Ate six red shirts from off the line;
Old Hogan grabbed him by the back
And tied him to the railroad track.
Now when the train came into sight,
That goat grew pale and green with fright;
He heaved a sigh, as if in pain,
Coughed up those shirts and flagged the train!

Author Unknown

Don't Ever Seize a Weasel by the Tail

You should never squeeze a weasel
for you might displease the weasel,
and don't ever seize a weasel by the tail.

JACK PRELUTSKY

THE FROG

Be kind and tender to the Frog
  And do not call him names,
As "Slimy skin," or "Polly-wog,"
  Or likewise "Ugly James."

Or "Gape-a-grin," or "Toad-gone-wrong,"
  Or "Billy Bandy-knees";
The Frog is justly sensitive
  To epithets like these.

No animal will more repay
  A treatment kind and fair;
At least so lonely people say
Who keep a Frog (and, by the way,
They are extremely rare).

Hilaire Belloc

FIGHT

Cat and I
We had a fight;
I hit,
Cat bit,
We quit.

Jean Jaszi

IF YOU SHOULD MEET A CROCODILE

If you should meet a Crocodile,
    Don't take a stick and poke him;
Ignore the welcome in his smile,
    Be careful not to stroke him.
For as he sleeps upon the Nile,
    He thinner gets and thinner;
And whene'er you meet a Crocodile
    He's ready for his dinner.

Author Unknown

THE HIPPOPOTAMUS

I shoot the Hippopotamus with bullets made of platinum
Because if I use leaden ones his hide is sure to flatten 'em.

Hilaire Belloc

GLOWWORM

Never talk down to a glowworm—
Such as *What do you knowworm?*
How's it down belowworm?
Guess you're quite a slowworm?
No. Just say
          Helloworm!

               David McCord

THE PANTHER

The panther is like a leopard,
Except it hasn't been peppered.
Should you behold a panther crouch,
Prepare to say Ouch.
Better yet, if called by a panther,
Don't anther.

Ogden Nash

JUNGLE INCIDENT

The tiny son of Marawambo
Met a tiger in the Congo.
The tiger screamed and acted wild,
But Marawambo's son just smiled.
"Mr. Tiger, old and fat,
You're nothing but a great big cat—
Scat!"
And that was that.

Russell Gordon Carter

DON'T EVER SEIZE A WEASEL BY THE TAIL

You should never squeeze a weasel
for you might displease the weasel,
and don't ever seize a weasel by the tail.

Let his tail blow in the breeze;
if you pull it, he will sneeze,
for the weasel's constitution tends to be a little frail.

Yes the weasel wheezes easily;
the weasel freezes easily;
the weasel's tan complexion rather suddenly turns pale.

So don't displease or tease a weasel,
squeeze or freeze or wheeze a weasel
and don't ever seize a weasel by the tail.

Jack Prelutsky

73

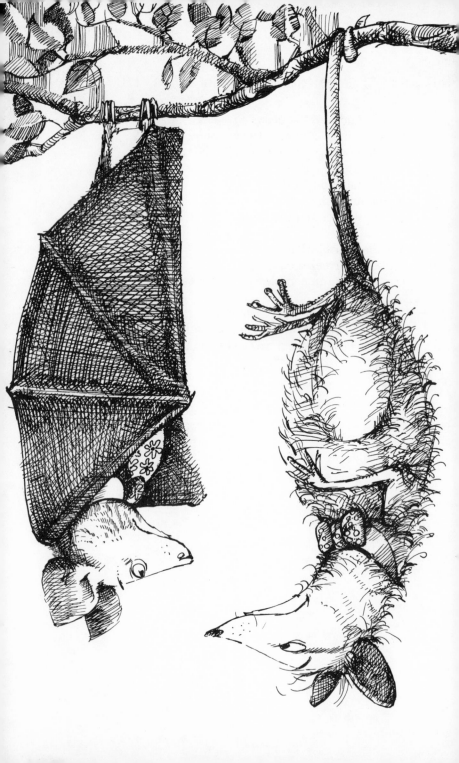

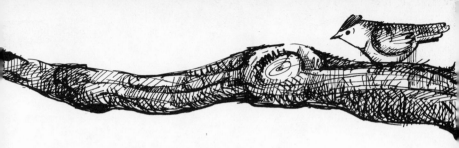

The Ways of Animals

POINT OF VIEW

The little bat hangs upside down,
And downside up the possum.
To show a smile they have to frown,
Say those who've run across 'em.

DAVID MC CORD

THE TALE OF A DOG

When my little dog is happy,
   And canine life is bliss,
He always keeps his joyful tail

               s
               i
               h
               t

               e
               k
               i
A-standing up   l

When my little dog is doleful,
   And bones are scarce, you know,
He always keeps his mournful tail
   A-hanging 'way d
               o
               w
               n

               l
               o
               w
               .

James H. Lambert, Jr.

THE FIRE-FLY

"Are you flying through the night
   Looking where to find me?"
"Nay, I travel with a light
   For the folks *behind* me."

John Banister Tabb

MARSUPIAL TRANSPORTATION

Dame Kangaroo is well equipped
With all the paraphernalia
So baby kangaroos can ride—
Hitch hikers of Australia.

Thelma Ireland

THOUGHTLESS GUEST

Although he's only asked to spend
The day with some admiring friend
Who has no room for so much Junk,
The elephant *will* bring his trunk.

Valine Hobbs

THE MONKEYS

Sing a song of monkeys,
A jolly bunch of monkeys!
Leaping, swinging in their cages
Looking wise as ancient sages,
Nonchalant and carefree manner,
Nibbling peanut or banana,
Every day is just another
To a monkey or his brother.

Sing a song of monkeys,
Happy, merry monkeys,
If you're ever tired or blue
I can tell you what to do!
Let the monkeys at the Zoo
Make a monkey out of you!

Edith Osborne Thompson

PENGUINS

Penguins with their chests puffed out
Blinking wisely, strut about
Hoping other residents
Think they are bank presidents.

Valine Hobbs

THE GNU FAMILY

Of all the beasts
　　Inside the zoo
There are a few
　　I never knew.

And it is strange—
　　But it is true—
There's *one* beast there
　　That's always GNU!

He may be old;
　　He may be new—
But new or old
　　He's always GNU!

He has a wife,
　　A good gnu, too,
And she is now
　　A mother gnu.

Today I saw—
　　Can you guess who?
Their newborn child—
　　A brand-new GNU!

Ilo Orleans

THE AMBIGUOUS DOG

The Dog beneath the Cherry-tree
Has ways that sorely puzzle me:

Behind, he wags a friendly tail;
Before, his Growl would turn you pale!

His meaning isn't wholly clear—
Oh, is the Wag or Growl sincere?

I think I'd better not descend—
His Bite is at the Growly End.

Arthur Guiterman

BEES

Every bee
that
ever was
was
partly
sting
and partly
. . . buzz.

Jack Prelutsky

THE WOODPECKER

The wizard of the woods is he;
    For in his daily round,
Where'er he finds a rotting tree,
    He makes the timber sound.

John Banister Tabb

THE OSTRICH IS A SILLY BIRD

The ostrich is a silly bird
    With scarcely any mind.
He often runs so very fast,
    He leaves himself behind.

And when he gets there, has to stand
    And hang about till night,
Without a blessed thing to do
    Until he comes in sight.

Mary E. Wilkins Freeman

THE GNU

There's this to Remember about the Gnu:
He closely resembles—but I can't tell you!

Theodore Roethke

TABLE TALK

Said Madam Goose to Mr. Pig:
"My friend, I really feel
You should be told you eat too much—
Your manners aren't genteel."

Said Mr. Pig: "Your kind advice
Is really of no use—
A Pig's a Pig you know, my dear,
And not a Perfect Goose."

Elizabeth Moody

THE FIREFLY IS A FUNNY BUG

The firefly is a funny bug,
He hasn't any mind;
He blunders all the way through life
With his headlight on behind.

Author Unknown

THE OCTOPUS

Tell me, O Octopus, I begs,
Is those things arms, or is they legs?
I marvel at thee, Octopus;
If I were thou, I'd call me Us.

Ogden Nash

THE RUM TUM TUGGER

The Rum Tum Tugger is a Curious Cat:
If you offer him pheasant he would rather have grouse.
If you put him in a house he would much prefer a flat,
If you put him in a flat then he'd rather have a house.
If you set him on a mouse then he only wants a rat,
If you set him on a rat then he'd rather chase a mouse.
Yes the Rum Tum Tugger is a Curious Cat—
   And there isn't any call for me to shout it:
     For he will do
     As he do do
       And there's no doing anything about it!

The Rum Tum Tugger is a terrible bore:
When you let him in, then he wants to be out;
He's always on the wrong side of every door,
And as soon as he's at home, then he'd like to get about.
He likes to lie in the bureau drawer,
But he makes such a fuss if he can't get out.
Yes the Rum Tum Tugger is a Curious Cat—
   And it isn't any use for you to doubt it:
     For he will do
     As he do do
       And there's no doing anything about it!

The Rum Tum Tugger is a curious beast:
His disobliging ways are a matter of habit.
If you offer him fish then he always wants a feast;
When there isn't any fish then he won't eat rabbit.
If you offer him cream then he sniffs and sneers,
For he only likes what he finds for himself;
So you'll catch him in it right up to the ears,
If you put it away on the larder shelf.

The Rum Tum Tugger is artful and knowing,
The Rum Tum Tugger doesn't care for a cuddle;
But he'll leap on your lap in the middle of your sewing,
For there's nothing he enjoys like a horrible muddle.
Yes the Rum Tum Tugger is a Curious Cat—
   And there isn't any need for me to spout it:
     For he will do
     As he do do
       And there's no doing anything about it!

T. S. Eliot

THE HAIRY DOG

My dog's so furry I've not seen
His face for years and years.
His eyes are buried out of sight,
I only guess his ears.

When people ask me for his breed,
I do not know or care.
He has the beauty of them all
Hidden beneath his hair.

Herbert Asquith

All Schools Have Rules

All schools
Have rules
Even those without 'em.
It's the rule of those schools
To have no rules,
That's all there is about 'em.

ELEANOR FARJEON

A MORTIFYING MISTAKE

I studied my tables over and over, and backward and for-
ward, too;
But I couldn't remember six times nine, and I didn't know
what to do,
Till sister told me to play with my doll, and not to bother
my head.
"If you call her 'Fifty-four' for a while, you'll learn it by
heart," she said.

So I took my favorite, Mary Ann (though I thought 'twas a
dreadful shame
To give such a perfectly lovely child such a perfectly horrid
name),
And I called her my dear little "Fifty-four" a hundred times,
till I knew
The answer of six times nine as well as the answer of two
times two.

Next day Elizabeth Wigglesworth, who always acts so proud,
Said, "Six times nine is fifty-two," and I nearly laughed
aloud!
But I wished I hadn't when teacher said, "Now, Dorothy, tell
if you can."
For I thought of my doll and—sakes alive!—I answered,
"Mary Ann!"

Anna Maria Pratt

GRAMMAR

At home it's "It's *me*."
At school it's "It is *I*"
And hippopotamuses
Are hippopot-a-*mi*.

Marie Hall Ets

SAM AT THE LIBRARY

My librarian
Said to me,
"This is the best book for grade three."
That was the year I was in third,
So I took the book
On her good word.
I hurried home, crawled into bed,
Pulled up the covers over my head,
And turned my flashlight on
And read.

But the book was awful
And icky and bad.
It wasn't funny;
It wasn't sad.
It wasn't scary or terribly tragic,
And it didn't have even an ounce of magic!

No prince,
No dragon,
No talking cat;
Not even a witch in a pointy hat.
Well!
What can you do with a book like that?

My librarian
Tried once more:
"This is the best book for grade four."
That was the year I was in fourth,
So I took her word
For what it was worth;
And I took the book back home to bed,
Draped the covers over my head
Turned my flashlight on,
And read.

But the book was dull as a Brussels sprout.
I couldn't care how the story came out.
It didn't have baseball
Or football or tennis,
It didn't have danger and lurking menace,
Or wicked kings like the ones in history,
And it didn't have even an ounce of mystery!
No midnight moan,
No deserted shack,
No great detective hot on the track,
Nobody tortured on the rack.
So naturally
I took it back.

My librarian
Used her head.
When I was in grade five, she said,
"Sam, it's silly to try to pretend
You like the books I recommend,
When it's perfectly,
Patently,
Plain to see—
Your taste and mine will never agree.
You like sports books—
I can't stand them.
I don't like mysteries—
You demand them.
You think fairy tales are for babies.
You hate dog stories worse than rabies.
You're not me,
And I'm not you.
We're as different as pickles and stew.
So from now on, Sam,
You go to the shelf,
And pick out the books you want,
Yourself."

And ever since then
We get along fine.
She reads her books;
I read mine.
And if we choose to converse together,
We smile—
And talk about the weather.

Carol Combs Hole

THE TEACHER

The teacher has quite curious ways—
She does not like the holidays;
She'd rather write with pen and ink
Than dig up worms and fish, I think.

Annette Wynne

A MATHEMATICIAN NAMED LYNCH

A mathematician named Lynch
To a centipede said, "It's a cinch;
    With your legs I've reckoned,
    That I'll know in a second,
Just how many feet in an inch."

Author Unknown

WHEN I'M AN ASTRONAUT

When I'm myself,
It's "1, 2, 3,"
I count
As I've been taught.
But in my
Space suit—
"3, 2, 1,"
Says the astronaut.

Leland B. Jacobs

How Foolish

I'm just a Monk and chatter a heap—
But I'm not as silly as some thinkle peep!

PETER   WELLS

I OFTEN PAUSE AND WONDER

I often pause and wonder
    At fate's peculiar ways,
For nearly all our famous men
    Were born on holidays.

Author Unknown

AS I WAS FALLING DOWN THE STAIR

As I was falling down the stair
I met a bump that wasn't there;
It might have put me on the shelf
Except I wasn't there myself.

Hughes Mearns

'TIS DOG'S DELIGHT TO BARK AND BITE

'Tis dog's delight to bark and bite
    And little birds to sing,
And if you sit on a red-hot brick
    It's a sign of an early spring.

Author Unknown

DON'T WORRY IF YOUR JOB IS SMALL

Don't worry if your job is small,
And your rewards are few.
Remember that the mighty oak,
Was once a nut like you.

Author Unknown

SHE WORE HER STOCKINGS INSIDE OUT

She wore her stockings inside out
    All through the summer heat.
She said it cooled her off to turn
    The hose upon her feet.

Author Unknown

SOME PEOPLE SAY THAT FLEAS ARE BLACK

Some people say that fleas are black,
But I know it isn't so;
For Mary had a little lamb
Whose fleas was white as snow.

Author Unknown

AS I WAS STANDING IN THE STREET

As I was standing in the street,
   As quiet as could be,
A great big ugly man came up
   And tied his horse to me.

Author Unknown

THE KING OF SPAIN

"I like this book," said the King of Spain.
"I think I'll read it through again."

William Jay Smith

Index of Titles

Index of First Lines

Index of Authors

ABOUT THE COMPILERS

Mrs. Brewton was born in Americus, Georgia, and was graduated from the State Normal School in Athens, Georgia. Dr. Brewton was born in Brewton, Alabama; he was graduated from Howard College in Birmingham, Alabama, and received his M.A. and Ph.D. from George Peabody College for Teachers in Nashville, Tennessee. He has also done graduate work at Columbia University. He is now Professor Emeritus of English at George Peabody College for Teachers.

Dr. and Mrs. Brewton have compiled a number of anthologies of poetry and verse for children, and Dr. Brewton has written many articles on education and children's literature. The Brewtons are folklore enthusiasts, and they both enjoy gardening in their spare time.

G. Meredith Blackburn III co-authored with Dr. and Mrs. Brewton the *Index to Poetry for Children and Young People* published in 1972. He has traveled widely in Europe and North Africa and attended school in France. He is a graduate of the George Peabody College for Teachers.

ABOUT THE ILLUSTRATOR

Graham Booth was born in London but grew up in Victoria, British Columbia. He was graduated from UCLA and received his master's degree in fine arts from the University of Southern California. Mr. Booth—author, designer, and active lecturer on the subject of illustration in children's books—has appeared on numerous panels concerned with children's literature and has won many awards for his work. He presently teaches art at Fullerton Junior College in Fullerton, California.

Graham Booth lives in Laguna Beach, California, with his wife and two young sons. They summer on an island off the coast of British Columbia, where Mr. Booth paints and scuba dives for relaxation.